Hidden, Lost, and Discovered

# MYSTERIOUS
# LOCATIONS

Rourke
Educational Media

A Division of
Carson
Dellosa
Education

ESCAPE

## Before Reading: *Building Background Knowledge and Vocabulary*

Building background knowledge can help children process new information and build upon what they already know. Before reading a book, it is important to tap into what children already know about the topic. This will help them develop their vocabulary and increase their reading comprehension.

### Questions and Activities to Build Background Knowledge:

1. Look at the front cover of the book and read the title. What do you think this book will be about?
2. What do you already know about this topic?
3. Take a book walk and skim the pages. Look at the table of contents, photographs, captions, and bold words. Did these text features give you any information or predictions about what you will read in this book?

### Vocabulary: *Vocabulary Is Key to Reading Comprehension*

Use the following directions to prompt a conversation about each word.

- Read the vocabulary words.
- What comes to mind when you see each word?
- What do you think each word means?

> **Vocabulary Words:**
> - catacombs
> - conspiracy theories
> - extraterrestrial
> - outrigger
> - prehistoric
> - quarries

## During Reading: *Reading for Meaning and Understanding*

To achieve deep comprehension of a book, children are encouraged to use close reading strategies. During reading, it is important to have children stop and make connections. These connections result in deeper analysis and understanding of a book.

 Close Reading a Text

During reading, have children stop and talk about the following:

- Any confusing parts
- Any unknown words
- Text to text, text to self, text to world connections
- The main idea in each chapter or heading

Encourage children to use context clues to determine the meaning of any unknown words. These strategies will help children learn to analyze the text more thoroughly as they read.

When you are finished reading this book, turn to the next-to-last page for **After-Reading Questions** and an **Activity**.

# Table of Contents

# Unanswered Questions

Nevada, United States

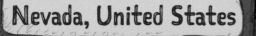

Paris, France

Rapa Nui
(Easter Island), Chile

ARCTIC OCEAN

ATLANTIC
OCEAN

PACIFIC
OCEAN

NORTH
AMERICA

SOUTH
AMERICA

ATLANTIC
OCEAN

SOUTHERN OCEAN

All over the world there are places with unanswered questions. How was this built? Why was this built? What goes on inside? Let's explore what we DO know about these mysterious locations!

Salisbury, England

EUROPE

ASIA

PACIFIC
OCEAN

AFRICA

INDIAN
OCEAN

AUSTRALIA

ANTARCTICA

# Rapa Nui (Easter Island)

Hundreds of years ago, a small group of Polynesians settled on the island of Rapa Nui. This island is popularly known as Easter Island. They traveled 2,300 miles (3,702 kilometers) to the small island in **outrigger** canoes.

Pacific Ocean

Rapa Nui (Easter Island)

**outrigger** (OUT-ri-gur): a beam with a log at the end that sticks out from a boat's side to prevent it from capsizing

# Rapa Nui (Easter Island)

Rapa Nui is covered in more than 600 giant stone statues called *moai*. The people of Rapa Nui carved these statues. We don't know for sure why these statues were created. One theory says they were made to honor important people who had died. Another says they believed the statues would improve the growth of their crops.

## Buried Below

Archeologists discovered some of the *moai* have a buried secret. Over time, dirt buried the gigantic bodies leaving only the heads above ground.

# Rapa Nui (Easter Island)

The biggest *moai* is 32 feet (9 meters) tall and weighs 164,000 pounds (74,500 kilograms). Some of the statues have another stone placed on their heads. These are called *pukao,* which means topknot. These statues have hair!

# Paris Catacombs

England  English Channel

Paris

Germany

Switzerland

France

Bay of Biscay

Italy

Mediterranean Sea

Spain

During the 17th century, Paris had a problem in the city's cemeteries. They were too crowded! To create more space the city turned to their old underground limestone **quarries**. The quarries formed tunnels under Paris.

**quarries** (KWOR-eez): places where stone is dug from the ground to be used for construction

OSSEMENTS DE L'ANCIEN CIMET

St. LAURENT DÉPOSÉS EN 18

DANS L'OSSUAIRE

DE L'OUEST ET TRANSFÉRÉ

EN 7BRE 1859.

They started moving bones from the cemeteries to the underground tunnels. They moved around six million bodies to what would become the **catacombs**. Some call it the world's largest grave!

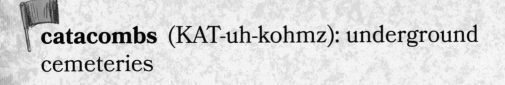
**catacombs** (KAT-uh-kohmz): underground cemeteries

# Paris Catacombs

A small section of the catacombs is open to visitors. When visitors enter, they pass under a doorway that reads, "Stop! This is the empire of death!"

ARRÊTE!
C'EST ICI L'EMPIRE DE LA MORT

## Illegal Explorers

Parts of the catacombs are closed off to visitors. Some people explore those sections anyway. They use secret entrances across the city. They have parties, watch movies, and map out the underground world.

# Stonehenge

Stonehenge is a **prehistoric** monument. The oldest parts were built 5,000 or more years ago. It is not known who built Stonehenge. Many experts agree that different tribes of people contributed over the years.

North Sea

Netherlands

England

Ireland

Stonehenge

Belgium

Germany

English Channel

France

Celtic Sea

## A Magical Place?

During the 12th century, Geoffrey of Monmouth wrote the tales of King Arthur. In these stories, he said that the wizard Merlin created Stonehenge. For centuries people believed his stories were factual. Magic was the answer!

**prehistoric** (pree-hi-STOR-ik): belonging to a time before history was written down

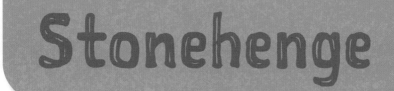

# Stonehenge

Another mystery surrounding Stonehenge is how prehistoric people moved the stones. Some stones weighed up to 8,000 pounds (3,629 kilograms) and came from 200 miles (322 kilometers) away! This was before the invention of the wheel.

One theory is that they used some kind of sled. Another says they made a giant basket. But no one knows for sure.

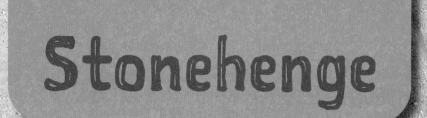

# Stonehenge

Most experts agree that Stonehenge was used as a burial site. But what else was done at this important monument? Some say it was used as a religious place, a spot for ceremonies, or a place where people came to heal.

# Area 51

Area 51 was used in 1955 as a test site for aircraft. But the U.S. government didn't admit that it existed until 2013. Because it was a secret, there are many rumors and **conspiracy theories** about Area 51.

Nevada

Utah

Area 51

California

Pacific Ocean

Arizona

## Google It!

It is illegal to fly over Area 51. But you can see a satellite image of it with Google Maps!

**conspiracy theories** (kuhn-SPIR-uh-see TH-EE-ur-eez): ideas that explain secret plots by powerful people

The most popular theory about Area 51 is that **extraterrestrial** life is studied there. This started partly because of a crash near the site in 1947. People thought an alien spacecraft crashed. The government said it was just a balloon with radar, similar to a weather balloon.

**extraterrestrial** (ek-struh-tuh-RES-tree-uhl): coming from a place beyond Earth

# Area 51

What is actually studied in Area 51? We don't know! What we do know is that it's secret enough that it has armed guards, 24-hour surveillance, and many warning signs to keep out.

# WARNING

## U.S. Air Force Installation

It is unlawful to enter this area without permission of the Installation Commander.
Sec. 21, Internal Security Act of 1950; U.S.C. 797

While on this installation all personnel and the property under their control are subject to search.

**WARNING!**

NO TRESPASSING
AUTHORITY N.R.S. 207-200
MAXIMUM PUNISHMENT: $1000 FINE
SIX MONTHS IMPRISONMENT
OR BOTH
STRICTLY ENFORCED

## PHOTOGRAPHY OF THIS AREA IS PROHIBITED

18 USC 795

**NO DRONE ZONE**

STOP

29

# Memory Game

Look at the pictures. What do you remember reading on the pages where each image appeared?

# Index

# After-Reading Questions

1. Why did the people of Rapa Nui make the giant stone statues?

2. Why did the people of Paris have to move old bones from the cemeteries to the catacombs?

3. Who built Stonehenge?

4. What is one theory about how prehistoric people moved the stones to Stonehenge?

5. What is one reason for the theory extraterrestrial life is studied at Area 51?

# Activity

Imagine you are interviewing someone who knows everything about one of the locations from this book. Which location would you choose? What questions would you ask?

# About the Author

Hailey Scragg loves visiting and learning about new places. She hopes to one day see the *moai* on Rapa Nui! Until then she will continue exploring her city of Columbus, Ohio with her husband and dog.

www.rourkeeducationalmedia.com

PHOTO CREDITS: Cover, page 1: ©inigofotografia; pages 4-5: ©Iuriii Buriak; pages 5: ©JoeBenning; pages 8, 30: ©Mlenny; page 9: © IVAN VIEITO GARCIA; pages 10-11, 30: ©Sergey-73; pages 12-13, 30: ©BeccaVogt; page 14: ©JonathanWeiss; page 15, 30: ©Nastasic; pages 16-17: ©XavierFrancolon/SIPA/Newscom; page 18-19, 30: ©NicholasEJones; page 20: ©SheraleeS; page 21: ©Dorling Kindersley; pages 22-23: ©cineman69; pages 24-25: ©shutterstock1405074776; pages 26-27: ©Grossinger; page 27, 30: ©Gettyimages1168262157; pages 28-29: ©BrianPIrwin

Edited by: Madison Capitano
Cover design by: J.J. Giddings
Interior design by: J.J. Giddings

Library of Congress PCN Data

Mysterious Locations / Hailey Scragg
(Hidden, Lost, and Discovered)
ISBN 978-1-73164-332-2 (hard cover)
ISBN 978-1-73164-296-7 (soft cover)
ISBN 978-1-73164-364-3 (e-Book)
ISBN 978-1-73164-396-4 (e-Pub)
Library of Congress Control Number: 2020945268

Rourke Educational Media
Printed in the United States of America
04-0902311937